Outlaw Psychiatric Slavery

Reasons for Outlawing Civil Commitment, Psychiatric Holds and the Insanity Defense

Outlaw Psychiatric Slavery

(First Edition)

*Reasons for Outlawing Civil Commitment,
Psychiatric Holds and the Insanity
Defense*

Michael Ten

Copyrights and Contacts

Outlaw Psychiatric Slavery (First Edition): Reasons for Outlawing Civil Commitment, Psychiatric Holds and the Insanity Defense

This is the first edition of this short book.

ISBN -13: 978-1494301439

ISBN -10:1494301431

Website: MichaelTen.com
Email: hello@MichaelTen.com

Other Publications from Michael Ten

All Adults Should Read This Book (Third Edition): A Book About Life Enrichment on Personal and Societal Levels (2013)

Attempt to Utilize Cryonics (First Edition): Reasons Why Utilizing Human Cryopreservation Is Ultimately Desirable (2013)

Acknowledgments and Dedications

I want to acknowledge and note my appreciation to and for my family, friends and others for giving me or facilitating the creation of help, inspiration and enjoyment in my life.

I dedicate this book to all individuals who attempt to promote and encourage peace, happiness and virtue on Earth.

Table of Contents

Preface

As far as I know, psychiatrist Thomas Szasz first coined the two word term psychiatric slavery. He wrote a book *Psychiatric Slavery*. Chattel slavery was legal in decently large portions of United States of America until about 1865. Chattel slavery is when one humans is forced to labor for another whether they want to or not. The slave owner who engages in chattel slavery benefits from the arrangement financially and economically. In psychiatric slavery, one becomes the patient or client of nurses, doctors, social workers, counselors and/or so forth, whether one wants to or not. Even when someone is trapped in a hospital ward against their will, most of the time, doctors, nurses, social workers and counselors benefit financially and economically from the non-consensual (forced) arrangement. Sometimes patients/involuntary clients might appreciate the experience and sometimes they might find it quite traumatic (as evidenced by the existence of the psychiatric survivor movement). Those who identify as psychiatric survivors are those who have be involved in the psychiatric system, frequently against their wishes, and have found it to be traumatizing, dehumanizing and/or torturous. It is through psychiatric holds, civil commitment and the insanity defense that one can become involved involuntarily in psychiatric pseudo medical systems.

This book is about why the insanity defense, psychiatric holds and civil commitment should be banned and outlawed. These are potentially a controversial subjects.

I want to note that I hope that we can have it be so that no human on Earth engages in suicide. I hope that we can have peace be ubiquitous on Earth.

Definitions

Psychiatric slavery is when a human in the role of doctor, nurse, social worker, counselor or so forth earns money and financially and economically benefits from having another human be their patient or client against that other humans will and expressed desire.

Civil commitment is when someone is involuntarily detained for usually up to about six months in a psychiatric ward/hospital. The exact laws vary from state to state.

Psychiatric holds are when someone is detained involuntarily in a hospital psychiatric ward or emergency room for usually up to about seventy two to ninety six hours. Again, the laws vary from state to state.

The insanity defense is when someone is determined to have behaviorally engaged in a crime, but found not guilty or guilty except for being insane. The laws and language vary from state to state. Often someone may either just be released and left alone despite having completed the crime or else stuck in psychiatric systems until psychiatric professionals deem them to no longer be a danger to anyone.

Introduction

I am writing this book so that we can hopefully live in more just and fair societies.

In the following sections I will attempt to persuade you as to why civil commitment, the insanity defense and psychiatric holds should be illegal.

I will also provide you with information about how you can help work towards changing the laws so that civil commitment, psychiatric holds and the insanity defense can be banned all over Earth.

Lastly I will provide you with resources for further reading and so forth.

What happens after one experiences civil commitment or a psychiatric hold? I feel that question is worth addressing here. That involuntary mental patient may then go on to eventually appreciate the involuntary treatment (this means that they either were feigning their desire to not receive psychiatric treatment or else they changed their mind about it) or they may never appreciate the involuntary treatment. One who experience involuntary treatment and never appreciates it may then go on to end their own life despite the efforts to forcibly stop them, they may live the rest of their life in misery and tragedy, they may join a psychiatric survivor movement or they may go on to find a way to create a life worth living for their own self and to live an enjoyable, fruitful and productive life.

I hope that all individuals who experience significant amounts of misery on this Earth can go on to experience a great deal of happiness during a long, purposeful, worthwhile and enjoyable life.

Consider Epistemology

Thomas Szasz who is the most recent human to voice a strong and courageous stance against civil commitment and the insanity defense repeatedly noted in his writings that he used epistemological reasons for as to why the insanity defense and civil commitment should be banned.

Epistemology is the study of knowledge and is a branch of philosophy.

How can we know anything? How does one know that sugar is sweet? How does one know that many trees have green leaves? How does one know that cancer often kills? How does one know that humans require oxygen to breathe? How does one know that zero is a number that can signify an absence of things?

How does one know that civil commitment is a good and just thing? How does one know that the insanity defense is a good legal tool that promotes justice? How can one know the converse of those things?

So, for example, in the following pages I will try to convince you that civil commitment is wrong. I believe that civil commitment is wrong. I am attempting to base my reasoning on logical and epistemological grounds. I hope that you will come to agree with me so that we can help transform human societies on Earth into ones that are more just, kind, fair and free.

Reasons to Outlaw Civil Commitment and Psychiatric Holds

The following are reasons for outlawing civil commitment, psychiatric holds. Reasons why the insanity defense should be outlawed will be covered in a later section. Psychiatric holds and civil commitment are similar enough that they will be covered together in one section. The main different between them is the duration for which they can be utilized. Civil commitment can lock someone up in a psychiatric hospital ward, usually for up to about six months. Psychiatric holds are of a much shorter duration can usually result in someone being locked up in a psychiatric hospital ward for a shorter time, usually for assessment or short term stabilization; psychiatric holds generally are for about three to five days.

Again, this section will deal with why civil commitment and psychiatric holds should be outlawed. Later, I will deal with the insanity defense.

It Is His or Her Own Body

In political debates about and in discourse over birth control and family planning, it is sometimes noted that it should not be politicians who can tell a woman what she can or cannot do with her body.

Death control should be respected as a civil right and no one should be able to *forcibly* tell an adult what he or she should or should not do with regards to dying.

Adults are allowed to utilize methods of birth control. Men and women can use condoms, birth control pills, have abortions and so forth. Adults are allowed to regulate when they procreate. Adults should also be allowed to regulate when they die, because it is their own body they are deciding about. With respect to creating life and giving birth, adults are allowed to choose what they do with their own body. Certainly, certain groups try to non-forcefully persuade individuals to behave in certain ways with regards to birth control and family planning; but with regards to birth control, force is pretty much entirely illegal. Unlike with issues surrounding creating life and giving birth, with regards to stopping living and one's own body, if possible, those with power when possible will not give individuals a choice in the matter (with regards to suicide), and will use physical force to stop individuals from exercising a personal choice (regarding suicide).

Death and dying is an existential, spiritual, theological and/or philosophical issue and adults should be allowed to make up their own mind about the issue, ultimately.

Death is unfortunate. I hope that no humans engage in suicide. However, with regards to suicide, adults should not be able to force other adults to not use their own bodies in certain ways, like dying. Although, peaceful persuasion certainly does seem an ethical way to try and affect others decisions.

Death Is a Theological and Spiritual Issue

If we want to truly live in a secular society that

respects authentic personal freedom, then suicide should be respected as a civil right.

Beliefs about what happens after one dies are theological and spiritual in nature. If one comes to the conclusion on their own that life is not worth living and that death will likely be better, then there are implicit theological and/or spiritual assumptions in this belief. Of course, non-coercive persuasion can and probably should be used to try and have it so that no one engages in suicide. However, force should not be used.

Suicide as Secession and/or Migration

Psychiatrist Thomas Szasz has compared voluntary self inflicted death (leave Earth) to secession[1].

If someone lives in Florida and hates it there, and decides to move to Costa Rica, it might be a good or bad choice. One individual who moves from Florida to Costa Rica might be extremely happy about having done so and find living in Costa Rica to be a wonderful experience. Someone else who moves from Florida to Costa Rica might find living in Costa Rica to be a horrible thing and even worse than living in Florida. Certainly, if an adult wants to move from Florida to Costa Rica, that adult's family members might try to persuade that adult not to move. They might miss him or her and not want him or her to move. Of course, they could not force their adult family member to not move to Costa Rica. If they did, then it would be kidnapping and a criminal act.

However, when someone wants to engage in suicide

and leave Earth, psychiatric professionals and those who are employed by hospitals are allowed to lock individuals inside psychiatric hospital wards and not allow them to leave. They are even paid for doing so!

The point is that if certain interpretations of Christianity are true, then someone might go to a horrible place (like Hell) for ending their own life. If that is the case, then forcibly extending their life on Earth (by locking them in psychiatric hospital wards) so that they might go to the Christian Heaven after they die, might be quite a good thing to do. However, if we want to live in a truly free society that respects personal autonomy, then it should not be legal to forcibly lock an adult in a hospital building who is intending on ending their own life and not allow them to leave.

Summary

If someone has broken a law, then they should be held criminally responsible and if someone has not broken a law, then they should be able to enjoy the right to be left alone, should they so choose. Civil commitment is used on those who are deemed to be a danger to one's own self or others. If someone is a danger to others, then they have almost certainly broken a law; and if they have broken a law they should be dealt with in the criminal justice system, not the supposedly medical psychiatric system. It will be good if no one engages in suicide and if peace is ubiquitous on Earth. However, using force to stop adults from ending their own lives is not moral or right. The basic logic commonly used to try and justify civil commitment is that someone who wants to end their own life is not thinking clearly and unable to make rational decisions; that is dehumanizing, and treating them as an object, rather as an intelligent human. Again, suicide is tragic and it will be good if they stop happening all together; however, only persuasion and kindness should be used to stop adults from engaging in it, not coercion and force.

Reasons for Outlawing the Insanity Defense

The following are reasons why the insanity defense should be banned and outlawed all over Earth. It seems that there will likely be more peace and justice one Earth once this happens.

The Insanity Defense Can Be False Mercy

The insanity defense should be banned because it can be a form of false mercy. Those who successfully utilize the insanity defense may sometimes be better off having not successfully been declared insane. Psychiatric drugs can have horrible side effects (and those declared insane and then hospitalized will likely be compelled to consume psychiatric drugs); and sometimes individuals who are declared or presumed insane are spend longer times locked in psychiatric wards than they might have spent in jail had they been declared sane. Of course, some who are found guilty except for insane, or not guilty because of insanity do not experience significant consequences for having engaged in crimes and having violated the rights of others.

The Insanity Defense Can Excuse the Guilty and Disable Justice

The insanity defense should be banned and outlawed because it can be a method of preventing justice and giving those guilty of engaging in a crime a free metaphorical get out of jail card.

The insanity defense should be banned and outlawed because the concept of insanity is not something that can objectively be proven or disproved. What is deemed insane is subjective. When one claims that deserve to be found insane and therefore not responsible, they have basically admitted that they engaged in the illegal behavior.

Insanity Can Be Faked and Real Insanity Cannot Be Proven

Insanity is not difficult to fake. Insanity can also not be objectively proven. Neither insanity nor any mental disorder can be proven to be a histopathological or pathophysiological condition; and both insanity and pretty much all mental disorders cannot be diagnosed using objective histopathological nor pathophysiological means, also known as an objective medical test.

If a human does behaviorally engage in a crime, they might theoretically claim that they were possessed by a demon. If that were truly the case then really, the human, who supposedly engaged in the crime would not objectively be responsible for their own actions. In the past, demon possession was thought to have been something that can happen. Some still think that demon possession can occur. Although the idea of having a mental disorder which has the effect of robbing a human of the ability to be personally responsible for their own actions is different than the idea of someone not being personally responsible for their own actions due to demon possession, there are some similarities.

The differences are easier to see. Hypothetically, in demon possession there is a spiritual entity that is evil that preventing someone from being able to take on personal responsibility for their own actions. That is in the realm of theology and courts do not allow demon possession to be something that can bear weight on the outcome of criminal court trials.

With regards to mental disorders, the theory is that there is a psychiatric disorder of the mind and/or brain that is stopping someone from being able to take on personal responsibility for their own actions; and because of this rather, than being guilty and then sentenced to experience a consequence like anyone who is not supposedly experiencing the effects of a mental/psychiatric disorder which renders one unable to embrace personal responsibility, one is deemed as being guilty except for insanity, not guilty because of insanity or some other verbal variance of this.

This is simply something that cannot be proven. Such testimony is based on opinion. Common sense is not complicated when examined and thought about critically and clearly.

Summary

In short, the insanity defense can harm victims of crime by having perpetrators of crimes excused from experiencing undesirable consequences; insanity is based on subjective supposedly expert testimony which is subjective by nature and not based on objective physical medical tests despite supposedly being a quasi/pseudo medical label; additionally, the insanity defense can be false mercy in that sometimes those who are declared insane would be much better off by going through the criminal justice system.

How You Can Help to Outlaw Psychiatric Holds, the Insanity Defense and Civil Commitment

Contact your law makers. See the resources section at the end of this short book for websites that allow you to find your law making and modifying representatives (at least if you live in one of the fifty United States). If you live outside of United States of America, then you must be creative to find ways to find your law making representatives.

You can also help spread these ideas to others, help persuade others that these unjust laws allowing for use of civil commitment, psychiatric holds and the insanity defense to be outlawed, amended and/or repealed and/or buy and/or gift to others books that Thomas Szasz wrote and other books like this.

Admittedly this book is less about how these unjust social institutions can be repealed and more about why. However, these suggestions are a good starting point as to how you can help repeal these unjust social and legal institutions and mechanisms. I think that if enough individuals believe rightly and strongly that psychiatric slavery should be outlawed, then it will be. I will note that I think that only peaceful and legal means should be used to outlaw psychiatric slavery.

I believe that through peaceful perseverance and through creative, peaceful and dedicated grass roots activism these unjust laws and social and legal mechanisms can be successfully banned and outlawed.

Conclusion

In this short book I have attempted to provide you with the rationals for as to why the insanity defense, civil commitment and psychiatric holds should not be legal. I hope that you have found these lines of reasoning persuasive.

I want to reiterate that I think that death is tragic and that I hope suicides stop happening all together. Until there is an objective medical test to determine otherwise, I also think that with enough dedication, perseverance, help and grit, probably all humans are capable of experiencing joy and happiness in life and experiencing life as being worth living. However, I think and believe that forcibly stopping individuals from engaging in suicide and trying to force adults to experience life as worthwhile and worth living ultimately probably makes the problem of suicide worse.

My views and opinions may change. I may hold a totally different opinion than what is in this book, as you are reading this short book.

In future editions of this book I hope to expand this book, to provide specific examples as to how psychiatric slavery is unjust and I also hope to provide more specific ways that you can work to help outlaw psychiatric slavery. I will admit that right now this short book contains mostly theory and general information about the topic. I think that you may be best served if you use this short book as a starting point. I believe that you do use this book as a starting point and do some additional research then you will find all that I claim to be true. This is the first edition of this book. While the ideas in this book in sound, in the future they can perhaps be presented in a way that is more appealing and convincing to more individuals. Future editions will likely be expanded and improved.

If you like this short book and feel that it is valuable and/or useful, please recommend it or gift it to others.

Notes

1. Szasz, Thomas. "Titles of Ignobility: Suicide as Secession." *The Freeman*. Foundation for Economic Education, 21 Sept. 2011. Web. 10 Dec. 2013.

Resources

Books

Fatal Freedom: The Ethics and Politics of Suicide

Suicide Prohibition: The Shame of Medicine

Anatomy of an Epidemic: Magic Bullets, Psychiatric Drugs, and the Astonishing Rise of Mental Illness in America

Why God Won't Go Away: Brain Science and the Biology of Belief

Ending Aging: The Rejuvenation Breakthroughs That Could Reverse Human Aging in Our Lifetime

The End of Poverty: Economic Possibilities for Our Time by Jeffrey Sachs

I recommend most all of the books that psychiatrist Thomas Szasz wrote.

Websites

Contact Elected Officials
USA.gov/Contact/Elected.shtml

Find Your Elected Officials
VoteSmart.org